Redux

B Bradford-Strom

BookLeaf Publishing

Presentation by *BookLeaf Publishing*

Web: www.bookleafpub.com

E-mail: info@bookleafpub.com

ISBN: 9789357441612

First edition 2023

To my children -

may you always bring me back

Parts

You strip me for parts
And I wonder what's going to be left
Tell me
Tell me
Tell me
What you need,
I would freely give everything

Tell me what you need
Tell me that you need something only I can give
you.
Imply that I'm irreplaceable
A rarity
An oddity.
It's all I want -
To be irrevocably special.

I want to be new skin and water,
An hourglass with infinity inside -
An entire desert and then the oasis too.
I want to be alabaster an onyx-
Opposition and compliance,
A deft motion or a shrugging gesticulation.

I want to be all of it.

When I say I want to be everything to you I
mean
Both the sun and the moon, the stars can be the
ashes
That scrape the sky when I worship you-
With my words
My lips
My embrace.
And when you turn to ash
I want to be the withered hand that throws you
into the ocean
And then the ocean itself.

I will bring the stars down with me in my sorrow
I will tether the moon in its fullness and then
watch it as
It waxes and wanes above me—
Rolling my tides into the shore
Slamming me again and again
Into the desert I once was.

And now
And now
And now
There is more life inside me than I can hold;

Than I can fathom
I cant believe
My body is a sanctuary now
A broken vessel is still a vessel
After all.

I am filled with potential
Meaning I've done nothing useful yet
Everything I say is a gauntlet to be won,
A victory to be etched into my armor
I started writing when I realized no one was listening
When I spoke

I am special strange
My feelings burst forth like a tangible force,
And I am consumed overwhelmed with compassion
Kindness clings to me like a threadbare sweater
Like a duplicitous act
Like deception Like a lie Like a wall
Like a warm embrace
I want to envelop everyone in

I am lonely lovely -
A stubborn weed that refuses to die

Pinched between two slabs of concrete
I fight and claw my way through the ground
Gaining purchase in city grime and chewed gum
once wilted flower growing softly,
Breaking the earth like a small bird cracks
through its shell,
Weakly
Independently
Awaited.

And now, I am a vessel, a ship
Carrying potential in my naval
Potential I could never fulfill
Potential I could never absorb
Absolve
There was no absolution after I left my mothers
womb
I want this seed to be a stubborn
Little flower, growing despite this

Parts II

I am filled with potential
Meaning I've done nothing useful yet
Everything I say is a gauntlet to be won,
A victory to be etched into my armor
I started writing when I realized no one was listening
When I spoke

I am special strange
My feelings burst forth like a tangible force,
And I am consumed overwhelmed with compassion
Kindness clings to me like a threadbare sweater
Like a duplicitous act
Like deception Like a lie Like a wall
Like a warm embrace
I want to envelop everyone in

I am lonely lovely -
A stubborn weed that refuses to die
Pinched between two slabs of concrete
I fight and claw my way through the ground
Gaining purchase in city grime and chewed gum

once wilted flower growing softly,
Breaking the earth like a small bird cracks
through its shell,
Weakly
Independently
Awaited.

And now, I am a vessel, a ship
Carrying potential in my naval
Potential I could never fulfill
Potential I could never absorb
Absolve
There was no absolution after I left my mothers
womb
I want this seed to be a stubborn
Little flower, growing despite this

Body my body
Growing and swelling
With round perfect limbs
And smooth, perfect skin
And to carry none of the trauma
I still house between my ribs
And beneath my chin.

Uncertain

My eyes feel like magnets,
Or, two planets, glowing orbs,
Drawn down. Drawn heavy
With gravity--the weight of living

I have been so full of pain,
The summer last, that I
Felt my existence, thick and unmoving,
As if I stood on Jupiter herself.

And now, oh, now
I am empty- hollow, my head
A gaseous dot in space -
So bright but dimming.

But I am a person, not a planet.
My heart is a slick wet thing
Heavy in my chest,
And my eyes are just heavy from crying.

Omen

I am full.
I am a moon bursting
With that borrowed light.

I am the ilk of a desert beast,
My hide, the trophy -
The reminder,
The souvenir of the pride
I swallowed to get here.

I am time.
It has burrowed its way beneath
My skin -
A warm ichor to grow in,
Or a viscous sludge to suffer through.

There is no difference.

You cannot hold me to the light
And see all sides.
In the sun
I am a prism

Of fractured ultraviolet.

But
In the dark
I am an omen,
Empty glass and hollow.

Houseguest

I am the perfect houseguest-
My face is schooled into mild amusement
Slight boredom,
I take sips of my water -
Always water - always convenient,
Tap my toe inside my shoe imperceptibly-
Laugh softly, like girls do
Not too loud as in excess,
not too loud as in
Forced

I am the perfect friend -
A brand new mirror to view yourself in the best
light
A little unstable-
A little too sensitive-
Like you have to protect me,
Sensitive, like you know better-
I make myself palatable
A courtesy mint
Easy to swallow
Refreshing

Refreshing.
I make my own lemonade -
Sliced lemons squeezed in water,
No Sugar.
Is this what I'm supposed to do with life?
Cut into the rind
And crush and crush and crush
until
Juice is dripping down my fingertips-
Stinging my cuts and callouses -

Is this what its supposed to feel like
To live?

I hand a glass to the people I know-
Here, I say, Here
Are pieces of me that you
Can't swallow whole -
A touch of sour
Watered down to taste.
Sadly, though,
No Sugar.

Stone Wall

I will stonewall my doubts
until they are nothing more
than the tide lapping against the shore
A tempest only when I need

I will bear my burdens
Not like a hero, but like a flower,
growing and wilting, then
growing again in it's own season

Because I am not a warrior,
I am not battle born and ravenous.

I am a question burning-
an ember in a fire so patient
so enduring-
charcoal pressed to diamond
stone heated to glass.

I am a daughter of divinity,

the worth so priceless,
the cost to match.

Cana

Stagnant water fills pots
yet they crave the taste of something sweeter,
the ichor,
the nectar,
the physical manifest
of these covenants,
supplications savored upon wine whetted lips

This beginning of miracles
a mother pleads
The Son-
He answers
The time is not yet

"Mine hour is not yet come"

But
it is the beginning
Small and soft as a secret
held between the teeth of servants
as they pass the water turned wine-
from a child basked in the water of the womb;
and as blood is the promise
so, too, is the bond it bears

Sylvia: Roman a' Clef

she called herself Victoria Lucas,
the penname used
to hide the public exsanguination of
bleeding a soul from a body

a roman a' clef for

the weight of the rocks in her pockets,
the imagery of bare feet on shore
and rough water calling her
to swim
to sink
to swallow the cold, cold drink

a traitorous body coming up for air,
blue lips kissing the surface over
and over
and over
until she let the tide bring her back

back to the bell jar and
the insipid reality of a shoe that hovers,
fills with blood,
but never drops.

and I never felt so much
like someone else
as i did when lying on the hospital bed,
tears trickling down the sides of my face,
filling my ears
until the nurses sounded like they were under
that same water

and the blood i lost the second day
after birth
and the gurney tracks through the snow
and the nights
whose only purpose was to interrupt
one long day

and the single drop of blood
on my bathroom floor
that i still won't clean,
reminders of cold, bare feet
on the tile floor
and warm, thick blood
from a body that refuses to die

so

People like her-
like me-
write.

we write,
hemorrhaging ink
on paper:
a type of suicide
we can survive
and be lauded for.

Glimmer

Loose lipped and mean,
look at those teeth glimmer-
Sharper than the rocks at the base of a cliff
an open mouth awaiting my free fall

I call her 'Monster'
she is swathed in shadow and bone
and uses chipped talons to scratch out a home
in the moments between waking and sleep

I often forget
that gore glimmers too;
Guts on pavement can still catch the light.

Each coin has two sides,
and she is the one that steals from her sister's
closet,
a wolf in sheep's clothing:
unexpected,
armed to the teeth

Depression,
My shadow -
Mimicking my movements in the light
Seething and slinking in the dark,

She lies in wait -

Watching me clench and unclench my jaw,
Rolling my neck,
Bouncing on the balls of my feet
Restless
Anticipated
Fists curled into white knuckles,
Crescent moons on my palms from broken nails,
Not claws

Some days
I feel I'm no match for her
As we meet in the dark room
Again
And again
And again

And again even as I dread the battle,

For my children i must win this war

TV

Television lighting
Is the esconcment of boredom,
The awareness of time.
Your skin felt like hours
Sliding against my mere seconds.
Your blankets doubled as forts
And tourniquets for protecting
And healing wounds
both seen and unseen.

I am not concise.
My words tumble over each other
Like waves on sand,
Interrupted or forgotten
Because nothing matters
When the world is as big as your
Room.

Retrospect I

I. Nitrogen inferior
To your blistering lips,
You took the gunpowder right out of me.
Sparks were a language only our tongues could
speak pressed against each other—
You tasted like sea salt and sadness and I
remember your breathing like crashing waves,
My skin was an avalanche of soft sighs and
shudders.
I was alive when I should have been dying.

Retrospect II

II. You were all blue,
you carried sadness like a noose around your
neck. We sat in the shower where I learned I was
red like my mother's temper.
Our bodies entangled each other and I watched
as the sky turned purple,like we were, together.
Purple like your sweater the first time I saw you,
when it broke my heart knowing you existed and
we could only ever be perfect strangers.

Retrospect III

III. It will always break my heart knowing you
exist somewhere that I'm not.
Because you are salve,
You are quicksand to my heavy feet,
And oh,
They are heavy.
This is the safest place I land,
And my heart is beating in an outstretched hand,
Veins pulsing, muscles aching from holding it
there for so long.
It's heavy.
This is the farthest from home I have been,
And your skin sends echoes
Into the cavern that I am.
I am.
I am.
I am.

Retrospect IV

IV.
I come back to this a lot
And I don’t mean it anymore.
I think the worst lies are the lies we don’t know
We’re telling.
What were we trying to save?

Children (for Bryan)

We were like children-
Our chaos brandished itself as
Crunching leaves underfoot,
And the imprints of the metal picnic tables
We laid on pressed to our soft skin.

The wind kissed us with a bite
When we walked, me,
Bundled in your worn flannels
And, you, forever with that fleece zip up
Bearing the burden of your backpack

It kept you alive

I feel like you knew you wouldn't make it.
Your eyes were too wide for someone
That never saw peace-

I remember the concrete balcony
Where we talked until we couldn't feel
Our toes, so we wrapped our hands together

And held on as we took turns
breaking and mending old wounds
They never passed our chapped lips

We were children-
And last night I felt your shoulder brush mine
In a dream of a crowded room-

"I thought you were dead".

I didn't see your face, but we sat this way
So often when your body was warm
And your eyes were still wide,
It had to be you.

Salt and Rain

You have not seen me in my chaos:

My hands are drenched in the blood of scorned
lovers
My heart is a black and writhing thing, oversized
And thrashing against my ribs

You did not know me at my worst:

When I was a flower bloomed and starved of
storm; My eyes sunken into the dark petals of
my skin.
And all The tears you caught with your finger,
were drops of Salt and rain I still tasted at night
when I cried alone.

You did not know me at my fullest:

When my belly was full of butterflies and
feathered things;
Light and effervescent, like soap bubbles
When chaos wiped her feet and left her shoes at
the door,
Visiting as a longtime friend

Confessional

1. I don't crave love
My arms are heavy with this thick skin--
no light can touch the bones beneath it.
I am an enigmatic sadness,
the extraterrestrial wisp of smoke that
curls around your tongue.
the addiction to loneliness,
I ache, but I am empty for it.

2. I am very afraid
these words,
they are an atom bomb,
the manners tethered to my sleeve,
i begin every sentence like a soft knock on
a bolted door.
I am here
I am here
I am here

3. I cannot be forgot
every footstep dropped,
every flower touched and held,
every shudder in the cold

reminds me of my need to be alive in someone else.
because being forgotten is a fear only had
when one does not know what
Comes after this

4. I don't know why
My promises break as easy as skin
turned to gooseflesh.
you ask me to stay behind with you,
fingers entwined like wires crossed
but I am poison in a golden chalice
and you drink me up.

5. I am selfish
i lean in and tell you this,
your shoulders raise in a shrug
and I feel my spine straighten notch by notch.
Uneasy.
I want you to love me.
I want you to love me
I want to unhinge my jaw
to swallow your offerings,
digest them and then demonize myself
for taking your life.

Recovery

I try out new words
To see if they'll fit in my mouth -

I am just full

Full of water
Full of something,
 near bursting
It wakes me up at night,
Trying to find words i would use to describe it

The blue dark
Velvet sky
Trees with limbs that reach and writhe
And a sky so empty,
Covered in a winter so bleak
That the snow would silence
A scream-

What is despair
But my body proving to my mind
That it hates how
Slow

Time

Goes?

Because I know
That my child will not wail into the darkness forever,
That the other will not throw her tiny body on the floor
And yell for no reason,
Or,
Any reason

Because I know
That the bags under my eyes prove that i am mother,
A title hard-won and filled with battle
That patience is a burden that i am strong enough to bear

For their sakes

my sanity takes a back seat
To the tiny smiles and thrashing limbs,
That every bite and slap and cry and tug
Is not my fault
But my responsibility

Because I know

One day I will recover all the things I can't find in this messy house
Like joy that isn't held together with ribbons of guilt,
Or,
Patience that doesn't leave me aching bone deep and crying in the shower

But right now,
It's blue dark twilights
And rubbing sleep from my eyes
And praying to God
For just one more hour
Of strength
Every hour

The Innocent

The innocent are by far the most inquisitive creatures of the Earth. Not because they are sheltered, or clueless; they are the sole population untouched by darkness. The innocent are not convicted. They do not leave their posts to touch the poisonous thing, but rather stand still in some divine purpose, some odd promise to something otherworldly. Their hands graze curiously over objects--examining, understanding-- touching objects and objects touching them. A gift of sentimentality to the unbreathing thing. The innocent must know, so they search for simple answers to the most divine things.

All the little trinkets and plush animals only loved because of the love for the giver of the gift. They possess the small act of possessiveness, owning what was never claimed by any other. Frightened, they always leave too early because of the confusion between knowledge and taint. Innocence gains knowledge, but the destruction lies with how that power is used. Once tainted--they seem to

feel the taint, the dirt of a misunderstanding
under their neatly trimmed nails.

That Night

I write like a person that existed once in a pretty little dream.
I write like the movies
And all their cinematic glory, held on the line between reality and working out perfectly.
Nothing works out perfectly
Or at least it never does when I'm around.

I looked at pictures and I used to be happy.
The smile I had, so fresh-faced, even with braces.
I was happy and life was good and then I didn't care at all.
There's still a note in my backpack from that relationship I ruined.
Just bunch of scribbled words that I could never bring myself to say.

I wonder what would've happened if I didn't
bend under all the pressure of a future
Planned only as far as the next moment,

But as I wonder,
I also wonder what would have happened if he didn't break my heart.

Forever was going to happen and it was in the form of any man who stole
My thoughts and wrapped me in his arms.
Forever was going to happen no matter what I did.

No matter what we all do, it will never be enough.
Because no matter how finite things seem, we are always infinite.
Infinite in the way we present our frail bodies--
Filled with fallible muscles and timid thoughts.

Infinite in the way we stole kisses from lovers
And hard candies from the receptionists at all of our doctor's appointments.
Infinite in the way that humans are--
When our bodies break down and we can't grow hair on our heads,
Or when our eyes turn yellow and our tears can't flow so easily,
What are we then?

I am not aware why I chose where I came from,
Or if I chose at all.
Sometimes, we just don't get to choose whose punches we roll with,
We just have to roll with them.
We just have to.

In this infinite way we all are, there must be a cycle.
There must be a time that we lie on the ground, and below it,
Standing up inside of ourselves
No matter how many tears we've shed.
No matter how many people have claimed to love us,
We must stand up inside ourselves and declare our own
Infinity.

The Quietest Sound

The quietest sound can be the loudest
When everything else falls silent.
Awkward, like the speaking dead.
Words falling from blue lips and clenched in shaking hands.

The smallest word can shatter the earth,
Only if it could manage to be muttered in the right ears.
Momentous, like the wartime changes that tilt the battle in their favor.
Limbs crumbling under foot like leaves in the fall.

Things used to be ordinary.
Things were ordinary before bathtubs held a new generation of dead.
Ordinary.
Before the youth had sorrows to be downing with the contents of red cups.
Ordinary, like the trepidation felt before twisting open a pill bottle and counting how much is left.
Now we hold our drinks at parties

And wake up with our pants around our ankles
with a stranger straddling us.

Unwanted.
That's all it is.
Unwanted pregnancies, unwanted sex.
Unwanted death, depression, wars, pain.
Unwanted sums it up pretty well.
It did.
You did nothing about it until the one you loved
looked in the mirror
And ultimately decided the life they had was
Unwanted.

The quietest sound is the loudest
When everything else falls silent.
Awkward, the word felt on my tongue
As I tried to speak around the lump in my throat.

The smallest word did shatter the earth,
When I managed to mutter it in the right ears.
Momentous, like the wartime changes that tilt
the battle to win.
"Help," came out of my mouth hoarsely like the
sound of chewing ice.

Help. The quietest plea anyone can make in a
world so unwanted.

www.ingramcontent.com/pod-product-compliance
Lightning Source LLC
Chambersburg PA
CBHW051745130826
49812CB00033B/1008
9789357441612